# Boa Constrictors

## and other Boas

by James Martin

Illustrated with photographs
by the author

Capstone Press
MINNEAPOLIS

Printed in the United States of America.

Capstone Press • 2440 Fernbrook Lane • Minneapolis, MN 55447

Editorial Director    John Coughlan
Managing Editor    Thomas Streissguth
Production Editor    James Stapleton
Book Design    Timothy Halldin

**Library of Congress Cataloging-in-Publication Data**

Martin, James, 1950-
  Boa constrictors / by James Martin ; illustrated with photographs by the author.
    p.  cm.
  Includes bibliographical references and index.
  Summary: Describes the physical characteristics, habitat, and behavior of boa constrictors.
  ISBN  1-56065-297-7
  1. Boa constrictors--Juvenile literature. [1. Boa constrictor. 2. Snakes.]  I. Title.
  QL666.O63M36    1996
  597.96--dc20                                        95-23098
                                                          CIP
                                                          AC

# Table of Contents

## *Facts about Boa Constrictors*

**Scientific names:** *Constrictor constrictor* is the name for the **boa** constrictor. There are more than 30 other **species** of boas.

**Description:** Boas are long, heavy, and non-poisonous snakes. The longest recorded boa constrictor measured 18.5 feet (5.6 meters). The anacondas, another constrictor species, may exceed 30 feet (9.1 meters).

**Weight:** Boa constrictors grow to over 200 pounds (91 kilograms), while the largest anacondas weigh 300 pounds (136 kilograms).

**Physical Features:** Like all snakes, boas have scales, eyes that are always open, and unhinged jaws. The color is **amber** or tan with dark brown splotches.

**Habits:** Most boas are nocturnal (nighttime) hunters that kill their prey by squeezing them to death.

**Food:** Birds, rodents, and reptiles. The anaconda also eats fish.

**Reproduction:** Boas give live birth, hatching the eggs inside the mother's body.

**Range:** The boa constrictor ranges from northern Argentina to northern Mexico. Other boas live as far north as Canada. Sand boas live in dry regions of Africa and Asia.

**Habitat:** Most boas live in moist rain forests, but some ground boas prefer hot, dry terrain. One species, the rubber boa, hibernates for months to survive cold conditions.

# Chapter 1
# Giant Serpents

Soon after Columbus landed, explorers reported that monsters were living in the jungles of the New World. According to these stories, snakes hundreds of feet long swam in the rivers and crawled among the trees. These snakes had eyes the size of shields and could swallow elephants in one bite.

The explorers had actually seen boas, especially boa constrictors and anacondas. While not monsters, they were true giants.

**A Madagascar boa lies in a grassy field to warm itself in the sun.**

**Boas are large, strong snakes that kill by squeezing their prey to death.**

Boas aren't poisonous, but they are dangerous. Instead of injecting venom into their victims with long **fangs**, they wrap their bodies around their prey and squeeze it to death.

Like most snakes, boas would rather hide than fight. Their colors make excellent **camouflage** and allow them to blend with their surroundings. The emerald tree boa is leaf-green for most of its life. The brown and amber colors of the boa constrictor make it look like dead leaves on the rain forest floor. Rosy boas have the colors of local sand and rocks.

When cornered, many boa **species** strike with their mouths open. Others, such as the rosy boa, will coil into a ball. They bury their heads in the center of the ball. They stick their tail out to imitate their heads. A predator will grab the tail instead of the head. This way, the snake can still fight back.

There are stories about boas or anacondas eating people. But most attacks by boas appear to be mistakes. From time to time, an anaconda will grab hold of a swimmer in a South American river. The snake will usually let the swimmer go, but sometimes not before the victim drowns.

## Where Boas Live

Although most boas live in South America, some have traveled to the far corners of the world. Two boa species live on Madagascar. This island is thousands of miles from South America and close to Africa. One Madagascar boa looks like the boa constrictor. The other resembles the tree boas. Their ancestors may have evolved as the South American species did. Or they may have survived a long sea journey by floating on logs.

Other isolated boa species live on islands in the Pacific and Indian oceans. A number of ground boas live in the dry regions of Asia and Africa.

**The camouflage of the Dumeril's boa makes it hard to see on the forest floor.**

# *Chapter 2*
# Snake Basics

## Lizards and Snakes

All snakes are reptiles. Reptiles are cold-blooded–they depend on outside sources for heat. Warm-blooded mammals, such as humans and cows, produce heat by releasing energy from food. Snakes, lizards, crocodiles, and other reptiles take in heat from the air or by basking in the sun.

**Searching the ground for prey, a Bolivian rainbow boa dangles from a tree branch.**

Snakes probably evolved from lizards. When lizards try to squeeze down narrow tunnels to catch rodents and other prey, their legs get in

**The desert-dwelling rosy boa inhabits dry, sandy terrain.**

the way. Over time, some lizard species got rid of their legs. This allowed them to crawl on their stomachs and hunt for food underground.

Some snakes still show signs of this change. Boas, for example, have a small pelvis–a bone to which leg bones attach. There would be no reason for a pelvis unless the snake's ancestors once had legs. The spurs on some boa species are probably the remains of ancient claws.

Snakes have one functioning lung. The second lung is small and useless. This suggests that the earliest snakes had two working lungs. As snakes evolved, the thinnest ones lived longer and reproduced more. To help grow more thin, they stopped using one of their lungs. The other lengthened inside their bodies.

## Other Adaptations

There are other **adaptations** that give snakes advantages over lizards, especially when hunting for scarce food. Snakes have plate-like scales that help them move. As the snake stretches out, the scales grab the ground, and the snake pulls itself forward. In addition, snakes don't have eyelids. Instead, a clear scale called a **spectacle** protects the eye. This scale helps the snake to see clearly while it is tunneling underground.

## The History of Boas

Scientists divide snakes into groups called families. Cobras and similar snakes are in the elapidae family, and vipers such as rattlesnakes are in the viperidae family. Boas and **pythons** are constricting snakes. They belong to the **boidae** family. Most of the species in this family live in the tropics.

Boas and pythons first appeared about 65 million years ago, near the end of the dinosaur age. Because they have some of the same features as lizards, they are called "primitive snakes."

Although boas and pythons constrict (squeeze) their prey, they differ in several ways. Boas give live birth, while pythons lay eggs. Boas have the remains of a pelvis.

Pythons don't. Boas have spurs by the **cloaca**. Pythons have a special bone by the eye, and their teeth are set differently.

Pythons live in Africa and Asia. Most boas live in North and South America. Scientists recognize about 30 species and many **subspecies** of boa.

The row of labial pits around a boa's mouth helps the snake to sense the heat of its prey.

# Chapter 3

# Hunting

The most famous boa is the boa constrictor. Its name describes the way it kills its prey. After catching its meal, the boa starts to constrict, or squeeze, its victim. Eventually, the prey suffocates from the pressure.

Boas catch their prey by pulling the front part of their body back into an "S" shape. Then they hurl themselves forward with their mouth open. Once they grab their prey, their curving teeth prevent the prey from escaping.

**Mice and other small rodents can't escape the tight and deadly grip of a strong constrictor.**

**Once the prey dies, the snake begins its meal.**

Boas eat almost anything they can get in
their mouths. Boa constrictors eat lizards, pigs,
and rodents, including capybaras. Capybaras
are the world's largest rodents. They run in
herds and grow to over 100 pounds (45
kilograms).

Snakes swallow their food whole. While
eating, the lower jaw unhinges from the skull.

The mouth expands around the prey. A boa can easily swallow animals bigger than its head. But it will rarely try to eat anything more than half its own weight.

Swallowing takes time. The mouth slowly wiggles its way around the animal. Muscles inside the throat grip it. Once inside, the meal creates a bulge in the snake. The bulge slowly slides down the snake to the stomach.

**The mouth of the snake expands to grip and swallow the victim.**

Digestion takes a long time. The cold-blooded boas like to bask in the sun after meals. They depend on external heat to help them digest their food.

Being cold-blooded has advantages. Boas and other reptiles need only one-tenth the food needed by mammals of the same size. Large boas can go months between meals. When food is scarce, boas have an advantage over mammals.

## How Boas Hunt

When human beings hunt, they use their sense of sight and of hearing. Snakes can't see well and depend on other senses. Some use smell. Others can detect heat. Some use their sense of touch to feel the vibrations of prey moving on the ground.

All creatures smell things with cells that detect molecules in the air. People have these cells in their nostrils. A snake smells with its forked tongue and with the roof of its mouth. The cluster of cells that detect scent here are called the **Jacobson's organs.**

When the snake's tongue flicks out, it grabs molecules in the air. When it returns, the cells in the roof of the mouth detect chemicals. They send a message to the brain. The brain then decides what the smell is.

The forked tongue allows a snake to judge the smell's direction. There are more molecules closer to the source of the smell. The fork that can detect the most molecules is closest to the smell. When a snake smells prey, it can extend its tongue and move toward the direction of the smell.

**An emerald tree boa curls comfortably around a branch.**

# Chapter 4

# Specialized Boas

Boas have several different ways to catch prey. Waiting quietly in the underbrush is the most common hunting technique. Some species use more interesting methods.

Sand boas, a group found in Africa and Asia, burrow underground. They have features that are useful for tunneling. The scales are smooth. The head angles like a plow, making it easier to push through the ground. Sand won't clog in their small eyes and nostrils.

**To trick its enemies, the black Russian sand boa has developed sand-colored skin patterns.**

**The garden boa is a tree-dweller. It will pounce on
its prey from a height.**

When ready to hunt, the sand boa pokes its
head out of the ground. The rest of the body
stays buried. It can smell with its tongue and
feel the vibration of animals moving. When a
mouse passes nearby, the snake explodes from
the ground. It seizes the mouse with its fangs.

Some species "see" heat. They have heat-
sensitive cells between the scales of their lips.

These heat sensors are called **labial pits**. With this heat vision, the snake can sense warm-blooded animals in the dark. Rainbow boas, tree boas, and one of the Madagascar boa species all have these labial pits.

The emerald tree boa lives in the rain forest of the Amazon Basin. It hunts among the branches of trees and shrubs. The labial pits on its upper jaw look like a row of fangs.

When at rest, the snake drapes itself over a branch in neat folds. When a meal walks within range, the tree boa flings itself off the branch like a spring. It hooks the animal with its fangs. Still dangling by its tail, the snake wraps the

**Even when tightly curled, the emerald tree boa is ready to strike quickly at passing prey.**

prey in its coils. The prey suffocates. The snake swallows its meal whole while still hanging head-down.

## Convergent Evolution

The green tree python of the Solomon Islands looks nearly identical to the emerald tree boa. Both are brilliant green and both have labial pits. Both species drape themselves on branches and spring into the air while holding the branch with their tails. But the python lacks the pelvis of the boa. Its labial pits sit behind the lip scales, not between them.

The green tree python and the emerald tree boa are an example of **convergent evolution.** This is the similar development of two separate species. If you are a snake hunting at night in the trees, it helps to have heat sensors, to have the ability to hang onto a branch when striking, and to have green scales for camouflage. As a result, one species in the Amazon and another in the South Pacific have developed the same features.

## The Big Anaconda

The anaconda lives and hunts in the rivers of rain forests. Unlike the other boas, it eats a lot of fish. Large anacondas even eat caimans, a South American alligator.

Anacondas may be the largest snakes in the world. While most reach only 18 to 20 feet (5.5 to 6.1 meters) in length, several have been measured at more than 30 feet (9.1 meters). General Rondo, an explorer and naturalist, once measured a 38-foot (11.6-meter) giant killed by Indians in Brazil.

Other witnesses have reported anacondas that stretched up to 62 feet (18.9 meters). A Brazilian newspaper reported that the army had killed a 156-foot (47.5-meter) anaconda that had knocked over cars and buildings.

Reticulated pythons, native to Southeast Asia, grow to similar lengths. But anacondas are thicker and heavier than pythons of the same length.

### U.S. Boas

Two types of boa live in the United States: the rosy boa and the rubber boa. They are the last survivors of a time when large monitor lizards, strange salamanders, bizarre turtles, and many other kinds of boas lived on the continent. The changing climate drove all but the boas to extinction about one million years ago.

The rosy boa looks like the sand boa and lives in similar habitat–dry and hot deserts.

**The rosy boa is one of two boa species that live in the United States.**

While some rosy boas do have a rosy tint, most show duller colors. Most have three stripes running their length.

Rubber boas get their name from their dark, shiny appearance. They live in the evergreen forests of the west as far north as British Columbia. They live farther north than any

other boa. Rubber boas are active in near freezing temperatures. They have even been seen moving in light snowfall. To survive the cold of winter, rubber boas become less active and make their home in a snug burrow.

**The Kenyan sand boa has amber and brown colors as well as a circular pattern.**

# Chapter 5

# Mating and Reproduction

$B$oas breed once a year. Until the breeding season, they live alone. When the season arrives, males approach females and courtship begins.

The female releases a scent to attract males. Often, several males arrive to mate. Wrestling matches begin. The winner approaches the female and stimulates her with his **cloacal spurs** before mating. The young are born about 100 days after fertilization.

All birds and most reptiles lay eggs, while mammals give live birth. Boas are

**ovoviviparous.** The female hatches the eggs inside her body. At birth, the egg has only a thin membrane. The baby boas quickly wiggle free.

There are advantages and disadvantages to live birth. If the mother carries the young, the babies will die if she falls ill or is killed. Laying her clutch of eggs in a nest protects them from the dangers she faces.

On the other hand, egg-eating predators may destroy the entire clutch. A cold snap or heat wave may kill the young, too. A mother who carries the young until they hatch can seek shelter from bad conditions or fight for her life and theirs if attacked.

## The Moment of Birth

Large boas give birth to dozens of young at one time. While most free themselves from the egg sac immediately, others die in the attempt. Usually some of the eggs aren't ready to hatch. Then the baby snake will die.

**At birth, baby boa constrictors are already one to two feet long.**

The length of the babies depends on the length of the mothers. Boa constrictors and anaconda babies measure one or two feet (.3 to .6 meters) in length at birth. Smaller boas give birth to fewer and smaller babies. Rubber boas may give birth to only two or three, although up to a dozen is not uncommon.

After giving birth, the mother boa abandons her brood. The babies begin to hunt and hide on their own. But only a few will survive to adulthood.

# Chapter 6

# Humans and Boas

Boas face many pressures from human populations. We hunt them for their skins and kill them on sight because we fear them. The pet trade takes them from their jungle and desert homes. As we log the rain forests, drain the swamps, and build cities, boas must squeeze into smaller and smaller regions.

Unless people decide to preserve habitat for wild animals, boas and other wild creatures will disappear. Boas have lived on the earth for

**Over millions of years, boas have adapted to their environment. But they may not survive the destruction of this environment by humans.**

tens of millions of years, while human beings are newcomers. The disappearance of boas and other species might mean the end of the human population, too. Letting boas and other wild animals share the earth with us may be the key to our survival.

**Whether tree-dwelling or ground-dwelling, boas are an important part of the natural balance of life.**

# Glossary

**adaptations**–physical features that allow a species to better survive in its habitat

**amber**–a light or shiny brown color

**boa**–a member of the boinae subfamily of the boidae family. Most live in the Western Hemisphere and give live birth.

**boidae**–the family of constricting snakes, the boas and pythons

**cloaca**–the vent at the rear of a snake

**cloacal spurs**–tiny "claws" found next to the cloaca. They may be the remains of true claws that snakes once had millions of years ago.

**colubrids**–the most common family of snakes. They evolved later than the boidae.

**convergent evolution**–when two species living in different areas evolve in a similar way, to survive in similar conditions

**fangs**–long front teeth used to catch prey or inject venom

**iridescent**–shiny, with rainbow-like colors

**Jacobson's organs**–glands used for smelling, found on the roof of the mouth of many reptiles

**labial pits**–spaces between the scales around a boa's mouth. The labial pits have heat-sensing cells.

**ovoviviparous**–giving birth by hatching the eggs inside the mother's body–a kind of live birth

**python**–an egg-laying relative of boas found in Africa and Asia

**species**–a group of living things that can breed with one another

**spectacle**–the clear scale that protects a snake's eye

**sub-species**–members of a species that have differences in color or structure from other members of the species

# To Learn More

**Arnold, Caroline.** *Snake.* New York: Morrow Jr. Books, 1991.

**Freedman, Russel.** *Killer Snakes.* New York: Holiday House, 1982.

**Gross, Ruth Below.** *Snakes.* New York: Four Winds Press, 1990.

**Simon, Seymour.** *Snakes.* New York: Harper Collins, 1992.

**Smith, Roland.** *Snakes in the Zoo.* Brookfield, CT: Millbrook Press, 1992.

# Some Useful Addresses

**Sonora Desert Museum**
2021 N. Kinney Rd.
Tucson, AZ   85743

**Clyde Peelings Reptiland**
Route 15
Allenwood, PA   17810

**National Zoological Park**
3001 Connecticut Ave. NW
Washington, DC   20008

**Toronto Zoo**
361A Old Finch Avenue
Scarborough, Ontario M1B 5K7

**Dallas Zoo**
621 E. Clarendon
Dallas, TX   75203

# Index